A CUP OF KINDNESS

Stories from Scotland

These five stories come from all parts of Scotland, from the wild and beautiful islands in the west and north to the small towns and great cities of the Lowlands. There are stories of love and of loss, of memories and dreams, of foolish people, sad people, and funny people. First we meet Jan, a man with a troubled past. Then there is Donald, a wise old boatman in the Western Isles, and after him, away to the north in Orkney, we meet Captain Torvald, Sigrid, and Andrina in a story going back many years. Then comes Ian, sitting in a police station, desperate to talk and confess everything. And last, there is Marina, a city girl in the right place at the right time, about to meet the man of her dreams . . .

BOOKWORMS WORLD STORIES

English has become an international language, and is used on every continent, in many varieties, for all kinds of purposes. *Bookworms World Stories* are the latest addition to the Oxford Bookworms Library. Their aim is to bring the best of the world's stories to the English language learner, and to celebrate the use of English for storytelling all around the world.

Jennifer Bassett
Series Editor

And for auld lang syne, my jo,
For auld lang syne,
We'll tak a cup o' kindness yet,
For auld lang syne.

Auld Lang Syne
Robert Burns, 1759–1796

OXFORD BOOKWORMS LIBRARY
World Stories

A Cup of Kindness

Stories from Scotland

Stage 3 (1000 headwords)

Series Editor: Jennifer Bassett
Founder Editor: Tricia Hedge
Activities Editors: Jennifer Bassett and Christine Lindop

RETOLD BY JENNIFER BASSETT

A Cup of Kindness

Stories from Scotland

Illustrated by
Dave Hill

OXFORD UNIVERSITY PRESS

OXFORD

UNIVERSITY PRESS

Great Clarendon Street, Oxford OX2 6DP

Oxford University Press is a department of the University of Oxford.
It furthers the University's objective of excellence in research, scholarship,
and education by publishing worldwide in

Oxford New York

Auckland Cape Town Dar es Salaam Hong Kong Karachi
Kuala Lumpur Madrid Melbourne Mexico City Nairobi
New Delhi Shanghai Taipei Toronto

With offices in

Argentina Austria Brazil Chile Czech Republic France Greece
Guatemala Hungary Italy Japan Poland Portugal Singapore
South Korea Switzerland Thailand Turkey Ukraine Vietnam

OXFORD and OXFORD ENGLISH are registered trade marks of
Oxford University Press in the UK and in certain other countries

ISBN: 978 0 19 479140 3

A complete recording of this Bookworms edition of
A Cup of Kindness: Stories from Scotland is available in
an audio CD pack ISBN 978 0 19 479283 7

Printed in China

ACKNOWLEDGEMENTS
The publishers are grateful to the following
for permission to adapt and simplify copyright texts:
Malcolm Macnicol for *The Pigeon* from *A Carver of Coal* by Eona Macnicol;
Calum Laing for *Donald and the Drovers* by Malcolm Laing; Archie Bevan for
Andrina from *Andrina and Other Stories* by George Mackay Brown; Curtis Brown Group Ltd
for *The Confession* from *Beggar's Banquet* by Ian Rankin; the Author for *The Day I Met Sean Connery*
from *The Short Hello* by Susie Maguire
Word count (main text): 11,205 words

For more information on the Oxford Bookworms Library,
visit www.oup.com/bookworms

CONTENTS

NOTE ON THE LANGUAGE

There are many varieties of English spoken in the world, and the characters in these stories from Scotland sometimes use non-standard forms (for example, the use of *ye* for *you*, and unusual word orders). This is how the authors of the original stories represented the spoken language that their characters would actually use in real life.

There are also words that are usually only found in Scottish English (for example, *wee* meaning *little*), and one or two words from the Gaelic, the Celtic language of Scotland. All these words are either explained in the stories or in the glossary on page 57.

The Pigeon

EONA MACNICOL

A story from Scotland, retold by Jennifer Bassett

The strong can take care of themselves. But what about the weak? What happens to a child, a young animal, a sick bird, when there is no one to take care of them?

Jan has found a sick bird, a pigeon. It cannot fly and is very weak. It will probably die, but Jan has a deep and terrible need to take care of it . . .

*E*lla was dressing in the bathroom. She couldn't get dressed in the sitting room while there were people around. And she couldn't use their bedroom because her son Robert and his family were sleeping in there. She called out to Jan.

'Can you find my best pink blouse, Jan?'

Jan went to the door of the bedroom. The door was open a little, and he looked through at all the clothes on the floor, on the chairs, bed, everywhere. Robert and Moira and their children were not tidy people. Jan wondered if he and Ella would ever get the house tidy again. He didn't want to go in and ask for Ella's blouse, but Ella called again.

'Jan! Are you bringing me the blouse?'

So he said quietly through the door, 'Please, Robert. Please pass me your mother's pink blouse.'

Robert said OK, opened the wardrobe door (which woke the baby), found the blouse and brought it across to Jan.

Jan took the blouse to Ella, who said, 'Oh, thanks dear!' in her warm, friendly voice, and he felt good.

Ella went on singing in the bathroom. She was very happy, with Robert and Moira and the two little ones in the house. Jan was happy for her. It was good that she had children of her own. He need not feel that he had disappointed her.

She came out of the bathroom in her bright party clothes. A big, good-looking, motherly woman. He looked at her with love, and she smiled back at him.

Then she cried, 'Hurry up, Jan! Get dressed. It's time. It's New Year's Eve. We're going out first-footing.'

He shook his head.

She cried, 'Why not? You came with me last year. And you enjoyed it. Don't you remember? You danced with me, and Moira taught you to rock-and-roll.'

'This year I will stay in,' said Jan.

He went into the kitchen, and from there into the scullery. The pigeon lay in a basket on a soft blanket. He thought at first that it looked better. Its eyes were open at least, round eyes like the centre of flowers. He looked at the little bowl of milk, and imagined that the pigeon had taken some.

But really, in his heart, he knew that the pigeon was now very sick. Worse than when he had found it seven days ago, on a ledge outside their bedroom window. Then it had moved its wings a little, trying to fly; now it lay still.

When he had first picked it up, the pigeon had not tried to escape. He felt sure it knew that it belonged to him.

'Take it to Jimmie Telfer,' Ella had said. 'He keeps pigeons. He'll know how to take care of it.'

'No,' Jan had said. 'No, it belongs to me. I am not taking it to any other person.'

'But you can't keep it in the house!' Ella said. Then she laughed a little. 'Och, have it your own way. But please, keep it in the scullery.'

She was a kind, generous woman. When he had first gone to work and brought home his pay packet, he had put all the money into her hands, as he had done at home. But her brothers had laughed at him, so he had stopped. But he still wanted to give her all of it. She was like a mother to him.

Now, like a little child, he decided to disobey her. He would not go. He did not want to go out among her large family, did not want all the laughing and shouting that they did at this time of New Year.

'Happy New Year, Mother!' 'A good New Year, Tom!' 'Archie – Andrew – Joanne!' Robert would love it, home on holiday. He and his mother could go out together and enjoy themselves without him.

They were waiting for him at the front door.

'Jan, what have you been doing? You're not dressed yet! Worrying over that old bird again?' Ella said, teasing.

'It's a *young* bird,' Jan said.

Ella laughed. 'Well, young or old, if you ask me, it's not long for this world. Come on now, Jan. You'll have to help Robert carry the bottles. I've the cake for mother to carry.'

Ella and Robert were waiting for him at the front door.
'Jan, what have you been doing? You're not dressed yet!' Ella said.

'No,' he said, shaking his head gently. 'No, I will not go.'

Ella did not get annoyed even then. 'Are you going to the pub then? Well, be sure to be at mother's by half past eleven. To take in the New Year.'

'OK,' he said quietly. 'OK.'

He waited until they had left the house. All was quiet. Moira and the little ones must be asleep. He found his overcoat, put it on, and went into the scullery again. He lifted the pigeon carefully out of its basket and placed it inside his cardigan, under his coat.

It wasn't strange to take the bird out, he said to himself. He had taken it out before. To the library, to ask for a book on the care of a sick bird. The lady in the library was very kind, very helpful. She had found a number of books about birds for him. But the pigeon was still sick. Then he had taken it to the pit, to the First Aid Centre, where Alec MacColl worked. Alec had felt the bird all over very carefully while Jan watched worriedly. But Alec said, 'It's nearly dead already, boy. We can't do anything for it.'

Then Jan went to the doctor's, but they seemed more interested in him than the pigeon, and gave him some medicine to make him calm.

It wasn't strange to take the bird out. He couldn't leave it in the house. He was afraid the children would wake up and go into the scullery and worry it. He had to keep the bird safe with himself. And he had to go out, he had to be alone.

Along Main Street there were crowds of people. And what a noise! He stood watching for a while. People enjoying themselves, having fun, shouting to their friends, 'Here's to ye! And what will the New Year bring ye, man?'

'Hello there, Sugar! Come on and join us!' Someone took him by the arm, and he jumped. He still hated it when people touched him suddenly.

'No. No. Thank you but no.'

Jan moved away, but others came round him. 'Is it Jackie Sugar? Come along in, Jackie man. It's New Year, it's Hogmanay. Come and have a wee drink for New Year.'

'Thank you. No. No.'

'Oh come on! Just a few friends. People you know.'

'Thank you! Thank you!'

In the end they let him go. He walked away down the street, but some more people recognized him, and a girl ran up to him. She put her arms around him, holding him tightly. She said something very kind, but he broke away from her angrily. She laughed, and ran away to the others.

His pigeon! What had she done to it? He cried out in Polish. Under the next streetlight he opened his coat. The pigeon was still, its eyes closed. But as he whispered to it, its eyes opened slowly. Then they closed again.

He began to walk up the road to the hill above the village. It was peaceful and quiet. Then a car came down the hill, catching him in its lights. My God, a police car! And they had seen him. The car slowed, then stopped. His heart began to beat violently.

A voice shouted, 'Hello, Sugar! Is this where your New Year's party is?' And then a laugh.

His heart became calm again. Of course, it was Britain.

He was safe. The police were only Angus Bell, and young Graham, who was a cousin of Ella's.

Angus and Graham drove on, and Jan put his hand under his coat, and stroked the smooth neck with one finger. 'They've gone away,' he said gently. 'It's all right.'

He was at the top of the hill now, looking down on the lights of the village below, and hearing distant laughter and music. Around him were trees and dark places between them. Trees were good for hiding in . . . if you needed to hide. He sat down under a tree; then came the sound of the church clock striking twelve. One, two, three . . . he counted in Polish. At the end he heard happy voices calling and shouting in the village, and then the song which Ella had taught him, where all must take hands.

But he was not thinking of Ella now. His eyes no longer saw the village, nor the shining sea, nor the bright lights of the town beyond. The lights danced before his eyes . . . the lights of another town, his own, the town where he and Hannah lived, where he went to work every day, the town where their baby Anyusha was born, and where she waited for him every evening ready to climb up into his arms. His own town, his own sad and broken town, where they had come for him because his great-grandfather had been Jewish, where they had come for Hannah and the child dancing in her arms.

He had to think. He had to remember.

The day when he came out of the camp, the loud soldiers who came to open the gates and set them free. He had found his way to Hannah's camp. The officer there had a list

'*Don't you remember a child? A small girl? Fair hair, soft smooth hair, blue eyes always laughing.*'

of names on the table in front of him. And he, Jan Szager, had stared at him as he tried to understand the words.

'I'm very sorry. She is listed among those who died. On the 20th September last. I'm afraid it's clear . . . The child? Was there a child? There's nothing here about any child of your name.'

So had begun his long and terrible search for Anyusha. 'Let me see the women who are still alive.'

They were thin sticks of women, with an emptiness in their eyes. It seemed cruel to question them. 'Don't you remember a child? A small girl? Fair hair, soft smooth hair, blue eyes always laughing. You could not forget this child.'

'I saw no child with her.'

'I never knew she had a child. She used to weep. But then who did not?'

He had searched for Anyusha for years. Until at last he had found a crazy girl. 'I arrived at the same time as her. She had a little girl in her arms.'

'What happened to her?'

Wild, terrible laughter. 'What do you think? They had no place for children.'

'You mean they killed her?'

'It was good to die quickly in that camp.'

After that he had come to Britain, found work here, made a new life for himself and married Ella. Sometimes in dreams he saw Anyusha, as a young woman, married maybe. With children. Sometimes he saw her in Main Street, looking for him. 'Is there a Mr Jan Szager living here?'

The dreams disappeared in the cold light of day, but then

the old questions came back. How was she killed? Did she know what was happening? How long did it take her to die?

He was dreaming now, sitting here under the tree. He had felt his child warm in his hands, warm and soft and round. Now he woke to find he was holding the pigeon tightly. Had he hurt it? He opened his coat and looked down at the bird. The eyes were closed, this time they did not open.

Then, suddenly, he felt a strong need for the village, for people, for Ella. He had been a bad husband to her tonight, to leave her to go first-footing without him. She had her son; but her son was her son, and only *he* was her husband. He had broken his promise to her.

His street was quiet and dark when he got to it. But his house was not dark. As he opened the door, light came from the sitting room, where Ella sat by the dying fire. She jumped up to meet him.

'You're the latest of us all,' she said. 'Did you walk a long way, Jan? Where have you been?'

'Up on the hill.' It was all he could tell her.

'Well, are you wanting anything before bed?'

He put his hand into his coat and took out the pigeon and held it out to her. 'It goes not well with it. It was too sick.'

He was ashamed to lift his head, because the hot tears burnt his eyes. 'I think it is dead.'

If she felt surprise to see the pigeon, she did not show it. She took it from him gently. 'Yes, it is dead. Poor thing. I think it had a hard time before it came here. Don't weep for it, Jan. It's only a bird.'

'Yes, it is dead. Poor thing,' Ella said. 'Don't weep for it, Jan.
It's only a bird.'

He said, 'I will not weep, if I know it is safely dead.'

Another woman would ask, 'What do you mean?' But not Ella. She said, 'It's dead, truly dead. Its troubles are all over.' Then she said, 'I think we should bury it, right now, in the garden.' She was wearing her nightdress, ready for bed, but she hurried into the scullery. 'I've got just the thing.' She pulled down a shoe-box (she had given him new shoes for Christmas). It still had the soft tissue paper in it, and she carefully put this around the bird, hiding from him the soft grey feathers, the rounded head, the round closed eyes.

'Now you come out and dig the hole,' she said.

When he had dug the hole and laid the box in it and filled the hole up again, he stood unable to move. Ella put her arm through his and gently took him indoors, to their bed in the sitting room, and lay beside him with her arms around him until sleep took away the dark emptiness in his heart.

Donald and the Drovers

MALCOLM LAING

∽

A story from the Outer Hebrides, retold by Jennifer Bassett

> *The Outer Hebrides are off the north-west coast of Scotland. These are the Western Isles, wild, lonely, beautiful islands – the Isle of Lewis, Harris, North Uist, Benbecula, South Uist, Barra . . . Even their names are beautiful.*
>
> *Many years ago there were no bridges between the islands, only fords. When the tide came in and the sea covered the ford, travellers had to take a boat . . .*

In the Outer Hebrides drovers were men who came to the island markets to buy cattle. Most of these drovers were farmers from the mainland, making the long journey twice a year. It was often a dangerous journey too, because of the fords between the islands. You could only cross the ford when the tide was low. If you were late and you were still walking across the ford when the sea came in, you were in trouble. Luckily, there were sometimes very small islands nearby, where travellers could sit and wait for the sea to come in, and go out again. A long wait.

Between South Uist and Benbecula is the South Ford,

with just one small island, a short way from the northern Creagorry shore. And that is where the famous story about Donald happened, sometime in the 1890s.

Donald was a ferryman, who lived in a little house near Carnan Inn, at the southern end of the ford. He had a boat on the beach for any travellers who had missed the tide. He worked as a shoemaker usually, but there were many late travellers, so Donald earned more from his boat than he did from making shoes.

He had never even travelled to the mainland himself, but he had met many travellers – different kinds of men, speaking different kinds of language.

There were the gentlemen fishermen, who spoke good English and kept their purses open. They were friendly with Donald, and he was happy to take them out in his boat, teaching them about the lochs and showing them the places where the big fish hid.

Then there were the travelling salesmen with their big heavy cases, which made the boat low in the water, and caused Donald much worry in rough weather.

Sometimes another kind of traveller went through the islands, looking for old songs and stories. Donald liked them because they were friendly and had the Gaelic. But weren't they foolish people, coming so far just to hear an old song about Fionn and Ossian, dead hundreds of years!

And the drovers, of course. They came west for the big cattle market twice a year, to buy the Highland cattle. Always in a hurry, the drovers passed through the islands, never once looking at the lovely mountains and deep blue waters of the lochs. Mountain, sea, history, song, and story meant little to them; there was no money in it. On the ferry they talked only between themselves, and only about cattle. Strange men, thought Donald.

In the evening of an autumn day three drovers from eastern Scotland arrived at Carnan after the ford had closed. To reach the market on Benbecula early the next morning they must sleep at Creagorry on the northern side.

It was nearly high tide when Donald left with them in his ferry. Halfway across one of the drovers asked,

'What is the fare?'

'Six pence each.' Donald's first language was Gaelic, but he knew enough English for the needs of the ferry.

The passenger held up three fingers. 'Three pence, that's all ye'll get,' he said.

'Ach, perhaps I'll let ye have the night's part cheap,' said Donald. The passenger quickly collected the pennies and laid them down on the seat.

Donald's pull on the oars was strong, and soon the boat was touching the shore. As the drovers got out, Donald pushed his boat away from the shore, and threw their pennies after them.

'Ye can have the night's part for nothing!' he called mysteriously.

The drovers climbed the small hill in front of them, only to discover that they were on a little island, and between them and Creagorry beach was deep sea. It would not be possible to cross the ford until morning.

The passenger held up three fingers. 'Three pence,
that's all ye'll get,' he said.

'Come back, come back, and we'll give ye a shilling,' they called out to Donald.

No reply.

'We'll make it two shillings and six pence,' they cried.

There was only an echo in reply. Donald had disappeared into the darkness. The sound of his oars slowly died away, and the soft silence of the Hebridean night came down, broken only by the clear call of a sea-bird flying overhead.

The travellers sat close together with their backs against a large rock. They were not happy men.

'We'll not get to the market early enough,' one said.

'We'll miss the best cattle,' said another. 'They're always sold first.'

'The best cattle in the Western Isles,' said the third, miserably, 'and we'll not be there to buy them.'

Talking was the only way to pass the time. There was nothing else for them to do. They couldn't argue; they had all agreed on paying only three pence for the fare. Now they could only talk, and stare fearfully into the sea-mist blowing up from the shore. They had heard stories of the wild men of Benbecula. And were there not ghosts in these islands of the strange language? In Uist, stories were told of water spirits, and of lights flying through the darkness, held in the hands of the undead. What a place to come to, even for the best Highland cattle at excellent prices!

The drovers had bought many Highland cattle over the years, but they never felt comfortable in these islands. It was hard to understand or speak the language for one thing.

What stranger could pronounce the terrible place-names of Sgarraidhleoid, Sliabhnahairde, or Bailenancailleach? No one, of course, except those who spoke Gaelic. Eilean Chreag Ghoraidh was the name of the small island where they now sat. It was clearly a place of ghosts and spirits, set in a circle of silver sand, with the sea all around. There was nothing to do but wait, wait in the cold night air, wait for the tide and the slow return of another autumn day.

Meanwhile, Donald had reached home and was warming himself slowly and calmly at his fire. He ate his supper, then said to Catriona his wife: 'Long enough' – long enough for the drovers to learn their lesson. So Donald got out his boat again and set off for Eilean Chreag Ghoraidh.

When they heard the sound of oars across the water, the excited drovers ran down to the shore, shouting:

'Oh, take us awa' from here, and we'll give ye a *crún*!'

Crún is good Gaelic for five shillings, and was very good money in those days. But Donald never asked for a fare as big as that, day or night, king or drover.

'Keep your *crúns*, you like them so much,' he said, 'but ye will every one put six pence in my hand before you put a foot in my boat.'

The drovers climbed into the boat, silently and thankfully.

Donald took them to the northern Creagorry shore, where the road meets the sea. He shook hands with each man and said:

'Goodnight to you. You'll know now that me and the boat are old but honest, not like drovering.'

As he rowed his boat home, he smiled to himself: 'Long enough, long enough – they've learnt a good lesson tonight.'

The small island of Chreag Ghoraidh is no longer cut off by the sea. On it stands a leg of the great new bridge. Benbecula can now forget the high tides and low tides on the South Ford – but no one will forget the story of Donald and the drovers.

HISTORICAL NOTE BY THE EDITOR

A concrete bridge across South Ford between South Uist and Benbecula was opened in 1942. By the 1970s it was becoming unsafe, and was replaced by a stone causeway, which was opened in November 1982.

Andrina

GEORGE MACKAY BROWN

A story from Orkney, retold by Jennifer Bassett

Ten miles off the north coast of Scotland are the Orkney Islands, wild and beautiful, beaten by the clean cold winds of the North Sea. Life there in the last century was simple, but hard.

Captain Torvald has returned home to Orkney after a lifetime as a seaman on the world's oceans. He lives alone with his memories of the past, a past he has tried hard to forget . . .

*A*ndrina comes to see me every afternoon in winter, just before it gets dark. She lights my lamp, gets the fire burning brightly, checks that there is enough water in my bucket that stands in the hole in the wall. If I have a cold (which isn't often, I'm a tough old seaman), she worries a little, puts an extra peat or two on the fire, fills a stone hot-water bottle, puts an old thick coat around my shoulders.

That good Andrina – as soon as she has gone, I throw the coat off my shoulders and mix myself a toddy – whisky and hot water and sugar. The hot-water bottle in the bed will be cold long before I climb into it, after I've read my few chapters of a Joseph Conrad novel.

Towards the end of February last year I did get a very bad

cold, the worst for years. I woke up, shaking, one morning, and was almost too weak to get to the cupboard to find my breakfast. But I wasn't hungry. There was a stone inside my chest, that made it hard to breathe.

I made myself eat a little, and drank hot ugly tea. There was nothing to do after that except get back to bed with my book. But I found I couldn't read – my eyes were burning and my head was beating like a drum.

'Well,' I thought, 'Andrina'll be here in five or six hours' time. She won't be able to do much for me, but it will cheer me to see the girl.'

Andrina did not come that afternoon. I expected her with the first shadows of the evening: the slow opening of the door, the soft spoken 'good evening', the gentle shaking of her head as she saw the things that needed doing. But I had that strange feeling that often comes with a fever, when you feel that your head does not belong to your body.

When the window was blackness at last with the first stars shining, I accepted at last that for some reason or another Andrina couldn't come. I fell asleep again.

I woke up. A grey light at the window. My mouth was dry, there was a fire in my face, my head was beating worse than ever. I got up, my feet in cold pain on the stone floor, drank a cup of water, and climbed back into bed. I was shaking with cold, my teeth banging together for several minutes, something I had only read about before.

I slept again, and woke up just as the winter sun was disappearing into the blueness of sea and sky. It was, again,

Andrina's time. Today there were things that she could do for me: get aspirin from the shop, put three or four very hot bottles around me, mix the strongest toddy in the world. A few words from her would be like a bell to a sailor lost in fog. She did not come.

She did not come again on the third afternoon.

I woke, shakily, like a ghost. It was black night. Wind sang in the chimney. There was, from time to time, the beating of rain against the window. It was the longest night of my life. I lived, over and over again, through the times in my life of which I am most ashamed; the worst time was repeated endlessly, like the same piece of music playing again and again and again. It was a shameful time, but at last sleep shut it out. Love was dead, killed long ago, but the ghosts of that time were now awake.

When I woke up, I heard for the first time in four days the sound of a voice. It was Stanley the postman speaking to Ben, the dog at Bighouse.

'There now, isn't that a lot of noise so early in the morning? It's just a letter for Minnie, a letter from a shop. Be a good boy, go and tell Minnie I have a love letter for her . . . Is that you, Minnie? I thought old Ben was going to bite my leg off then. Yes, Minnie, a fine morning, it is that . . .'

I have never liked that postman – he is only interested in people that he thinks are important in the island – but that morning he came past my window like a messenger of light. He opened the door without knocking (I am not an important person). He said, 'Letter from far away, Captain.' He put the letter on the chair nearest the door.

I was opening my mouth to say, 'I'm not very well. I wonder . . .' But if any words came out, they were only ghostly whispers.

Stanley looked at the dead fire and the closed window. He said, 'Phew! It's airless in here, Captain. You want to get some fresh air . . .' Then he went, closing the door behind him. (No message would go to Andrina, then, or to the doctor in the village.)

I thought, until I slept again, about the last letter people write before dying . . .

In a day or two, of course, I was all right again; a tough old sailor like me isn't killed off that easily.

But there was a sadness, a loneliness around me. I had been ill, alone, helpless. Why had my friend left me in my bad time?

Then I became sensible again. 'Torvald, you old fool,' I said to myself. 'Why should a pretty twenty-year-old spend her time with you? Look at it this way, man – you've had a winter of her kindness and care. She brought a lamp into your dark time; ever since the Harvest Home party when (like a fool) you had too much whisky. And she helped you home and put you into bed . . . Well, for some reason or another Andrina hasn't been able to come these last few days. I'll find out, today, the reason.'

It was time for me to get to the village. There was not a piece of bread or a gram of butter in the cupboard. The shop

'Letter from far away, Captain,' said Stanley.
He put the letter on the chair nearest the door.

was also the Post Office – I had to collect two weeks' pension. I promised myself a beer or two in the pub, to wash the last of that sickness out of me.

I realized, as I slowly walked those two miles, that I knew nothing about Andrina at all. I had never asked, and she had said nothing. What was her father? Had she sisters and brothers? I had never even learned in our talks where she lived on the island. It was enough that she came every evening, soon after sunset, did her quiet work in the house, and stayed a while; and left a peace behind – a feeling that a clean summer wind had blown through the heart of the house, bringing light and sweetness.

But the girl had never stopped, all last winter, asking me questions about myself – all the good and bad and exciting things that had happened to me. Of course I told her this and that. Old men love to make their past important, to make a simple life sound full of interest and great success. I gave her stories in which I was a wild, brave seaman, who was known and feared across all the seas of the world, from Hong Kong to Durban to San Francisco. Oh, what a famous sea captain I was!

And the girl loved these stories, true or not true, turning the lamp down a little, to make everything more mysterious, stirring the fire into new flowers of flame . . .

One story I did not tell her. It is the time in my life that hurts me every time I think of it. I don't think of it often, because that time is locked up and the key is dropped deep in the Atlantic Ocean, but it is a ghost, as I said earlier, that woke during my recent illness.

On her last evening at my fireside I did, I know, tell a little of that story, just a few half-ashamed pieces of it.

Suddenly, before I had finished – did she already know the ending? – she had put a white look and a cold kiss on my cheek, and gone out at the door; as I learned later, for the last time.

Hurt or no, I will tell the story here and now. You who look and listen are not Andrina – to you it will seem a story of rough country people, a story of the young and foolish, the young and heartless.

In the island, fifty years ago, a young man and a young woman came together. They had known each other all their lives up to then, of course – they had sat in the school room together – but on one day in early summer this boy from one croft and this girl from another distant croft looked at each other with new eyes.

After the midsummer dance at the big house, they walked together across the hill under the wide summer night sky – it is never dark here in summertime – and came to the rocks and the sand and sea just as the sun was rising. For an hour or more they stayed there, held in the magic of that time, while the sea and the sunlight danced around them.

It was a story full of the light of a single short summer. The boy and the girl lived, it seemed, on each other's heartbeats. Their parents' crofts were miles distant, but they managed to meet most days; at the crossroads, at the village shop, on the side of the hill. But really those places were too open, there were too many windows – so their feet went secretly night after night to the beach with its bird-cries, its cave, its changing waters. There they could be safely alone, no one to see the gentle touches of hand and mouth, no one to hear the words that were nonsense but that became in his mouth a sweet mysterious music . . . 'Sigrid.'

The boy – his future, once the magic of this summer was over, was to go to the university in Aberdeen and there study to be a man of importance and riches, far from the simple life of a croft.

No door like that would open for Sigrid. Her future was the small family croft, the digging of peat, the making of butter and cheese. But for a short time only. Her place would be beside the young man whose heartbeats she lived on, when he had finished his studies and become a teacher. They walked day after day beside the shining waters.

But one evening, at the cave, towards the end of that summer, when the fields were turning golden, she had something to tell him – a frightened, dangerous, secret thing. And at once the summertime magic was broken. He shook his head. He looked away. He looked at her again as a stranger, a cruel hateful look. She put out her hand to him, shaking a little. He pushed her away. He turned. He ran up the beach and along the path to the road above; and the golden fields closed round him and hid him from her.

And the girl was left alone at the mouth of the cave, with an even greater loneliness in the mystery ahead of her.

The young man did not go to any university. That same day he was in Hamnavoe, asking for an immediate ticket on a ship to Canada, Australia, South Africa – anywhere.

*They went secretly night after night to the beach with its bird-cries,
its cave, its changing waters.*

After that the story became still more cruel and still more sad. The girl followed him across the Atlantic a month or so later, but discovered that he had already gone from that place. He had taken work as a seaman on a ship sailing to the other side of the world. So she was told, and she was more lost and lonely than ever.

For the next fifty years, that was his life: making salt circles around the world, with no home anywhere. True, he studied, became a ship's officer, and finally a captain. But the empty years became too long, too heavy. There is a time, when white hairs come, to turn your back on your life's work. That is what the seaman did, and he came home to his island, hoping that fifty winters would be enough to bury the past in forgetfulness.

And so it was, or seemed to be. One or two people half-remembered him. The name of a woman who had been young fifty years before was not spoken, neither by him nor by other people. Her parents' croft was gone, was now just a pile of stones on the side of the hill. He climbed up to it one day and looked at it coldly. No sweet ghost stood waiting at the end of the house, waiting for the evening call – 'Sigrid . . .'

❧

I collected my pension, and a basket full of food, in the village shop. Tina Stewart the postmistress knew everybody and everything; the complete family history of everybody in the island. I tried different ways of getting information from her. What was new or strange in the island? Had anyone been taken suddenly ill? Had anybody – a young woman, for example – had to leave the island suddenly, for whatever reason?

The sharp eyes of Miss Stewart stared at me long and hard. No, said she, she had never known the island quieter. Nobody had come or gone.

'Only yourself, Captain Torvald, you have been ill in bed, I hear. You should take good care of yourself, you all alone up there. There's still a greyness in your face . . .'

I said I was sorry to take up her time. Somebody had spoken a name to me – Andrina. It was not important, but could Miss Stewart tell me which farm or croft this Andrina came from?

Tina Stewart looked at me a long while, then shook her head. There was nobody of that name – woman or girl or child – in the island; and there never had been, she was sure of it.

I paid for my shopping, with shaking fingers, and left.

I felt the need of a drink. In the pub Isaac Irving stood behind the bar. There were two fishermen at the far end, next to the fire, drinking their beer.

I said, after the third whisky, 'Look, Isaac, I suppose everyone in the island knows that Andrina – that girl – has been coming all winter up to my place, to do a bit of cleaning and washing and cooking for me. She hasn't been for a week now and more. Do you know if there's anything the matter with her?' (I was afraid that Andrina had suddenly fallen in love, and that love now filled her life, leaving no time for small kindnesses.)

Isaac stared at me. He seemed to think I was mad. 'A

Isaac stared at me. 'How many whiskies did you have
before you came here, Captain, eh?'

young woman,' said he. 'A young woman up at your house?
A home help, is she? I didn't know you had a home help.
How many whiskies did you have before you came here,
Captain, eh?' And he turned to smile at the two fishermen
over by the fire.

I drank down my fourth whisky and prepared to go.

'Sorry, Captain,' Isaac Irving called after me. 'I think you
imagined that girl, when the fever was on you. Sometimes
that happens. I never have fever dreams like that. You're
lucky, Captain – a sweet thing like Andrina!'

I could not begin to understand. Isaac Irving knows the
island and its people even better than Tina Stewart. And he
is a kindly man. Why would he make fun of me?

Going home, March winds were moving over the island.
The sky was taller and bluer. Flowers among the rocks spoke
silently of the coming of spring. A young lamb danced, all
four feet in the air at once.

I found, lying on the table, unopened, the letter that had
arrived three mornings ago. It had come from Australia,
posted last October.

I followed you half round the world when you ran
from Selskay fifty years ago. But I stopped at last in
Tasmania, knowing it was useless for me to continue
following you. I have kept a silence too, because of my
great love for you. I did not want you to feel the pain
that I had felt, in many ways, over the years. We are
both old, maybe this letter will never find you; perhaps

you never returned to Selskay, perhaps you have died and are now only dust in the earth or salt in the sea.

I think, if you are still alive and (it may be) lonely, that my news will bring you happiness, although the end of it is sadness, like so much of life. Of your child – our child – I do not say anything, because you did not wish to accept her. But that child had, in her turn, a daughter, and I do not think that I have seen so sweet a girl in all my days. I thank you for giving me (although you did not choose to) that light and goodness in my last years. She wanted to be a lamp in your winter, too, because I often spoke about you and the long-gone summer that we had together, which was, to me at least, so wonderful. I told her nothing of the end of that time, that you and some others thought to be shameful. I told her only things that came sweetly from my mouth.

And she used to say, often, 'I wish I knew that grandfather of mine. Gran, do you think he's lonely? I wish I could make him a pot of tea and see to his fire. Some day I'm going to Scotland and I'm going to knock on his door, and I'll do things for him. Did you love him very much, Gran? He must be a good person, that old sailor, because you loved him. I *will* see him. I'll hear the old stories from his own mouth. Most of all, of course, the love story – because you, Gran, tell me nothing about that . . .'

I am writing this letter, Bill, to tell you that this can now never be. Our granddaughter Andrina died last week, suddenly, in the first days of spring . . .

Later, over the fire, I thought of the brightness and the cheer that visitor had brought to my latest winter, night after night; and of how she had always come with the first shadows and the first star; but there, where she was dust, a new time was brightening earth and sea.

NOTE BY THE EDITOR
The island name 'Selskay' is not actually found in Orkney; it is a name invented by George Mackay Brown. He also used 'Hamnavoe', which is an old Norse word, for the town of Stromness.

The Confession

IAN RANKIN

A story from Scotland, retold by Jennifer Bassett

When a criminal is arrested, one of the first things that happens is the interview at the police station. Questions, and answers. The detective asks the questions, and the criminal answers – or not. Some of them won't say a word; others talk and talk . . . and talk.

Ian is a great talker. He wants to tell the detective everything, from beginning to end, every single detail . . .

'It was Tony's idea,' Ian says, moving about in his seat. 'Tony's my brother, two years younger than me, but he was always the clever one. It was all his idea. I just went along with it.'

He's still trying to get comfortable. It's not easy to get comfortable in the interview room. The detective could tell him that. He could tell him about the chair he's sitting in. It's a special interview chair, with its front legs just a little bit shorter than its back legs. Very uncomfortable.

'So Tony says to me one day, he says: "Ian, this is one plan that cannot fail." And he tells me about it. We spend a long time talking about it, and I'm trying to find things wrong with it, but it's good, it's a really good plan. That's why I'm here. It was just too good . . .'

Ian looks around again, studying the walls, looking for two-way mirrors, secret listening spy holes. The one thing he hasn't expected is the quietness. It's eleven-thirty on a weekday night, and the police station is like a ghost town. Ian wants to see lights, action, lots of police uniforms. Yet again in his life, he's disappointed. He goes on with his story.

Tony had noticed the slip-road. He drove from Fife to Edinburgh most Saturday nights, taking a car full of friends for a night out. On the A90 road south of the Forth Road Bridge, Tony saw the signpost for the slip-road:

DEPARTMENT OF TRANSPORT
VEHICLE CHECK AREA ONLY

That's what started his idea. The next morning he went back and drove up the slip-road, which took him to a kind of roundabout in the middle of nowhere. He stopped his car and got out. There was grass growing in the middle of the road. He didn't think the place got used much. There was a hut nearby, and another slip-road went back down on to the A90 road. He stood there for a while, listening to the noise of traffic below him, and the idea slowly grew in his mind.

'You see,' Ian went on, 'Tony had two guard's uniforms at home. He's always had the idea of robbing some place, and always knew those uniforms would be useful. And one of his old friends, a man called Malc, was good at getting false papers, so Tony brought him in. Have you got a cigarette?'

The detective points to the NO SMOKING sign, but then

raises his eyebrows, and says, 'OK.' He gives Ian a packet of ten and some matches.

'Thanks.' Ian lights up a cigarette, breathes noisily. 'So you see,' he goes on, 'it was all Tony's idea, and Malc, well, he'd done this kind of thing before. I was just family, that's why Tony brought me in. I'm not saying I wasn't part of it. I mean, that's why I'm here now. I just want it in the police report that I wasn't the leader, the clever one.'

'I think I can agree with that,' the detective says.

'Aren't you going to write all this down?' asks Ian.

'We're trained, boy. We remember everything.'

So Ian nods, goes on with his story. The interview room is small and airless. It smells of all the people who have told their stories in there. A few of the stories were even true . . .

'So we drive up this slip-road a few times. Nobody notices us, asks what we're doing. Tony's happy about that, and the plan is fixed for last Wednesday.'

'Why a Wednesday?' the detective asks.

Ian shakes his head. 'Tony's idea,' he said. He moves around again in his chair, remembering Wednesday night.

Tony and Ian were dressed in the uniforms. Tony had a friend with a big truck. It had been easy to borrow it for the night. The story was, they were helping someone move house. They took the truck up to the roundabout, left the car near the bottom of the slip-road. Malc was dressed like a truck driver, and he and Ian waited by the truck. Tony went back down to the A90, stood by the Department of Transport sign, and used a torch to stop a lorry on the road. Then he told the lorry driver to drive up the slip-road, to the

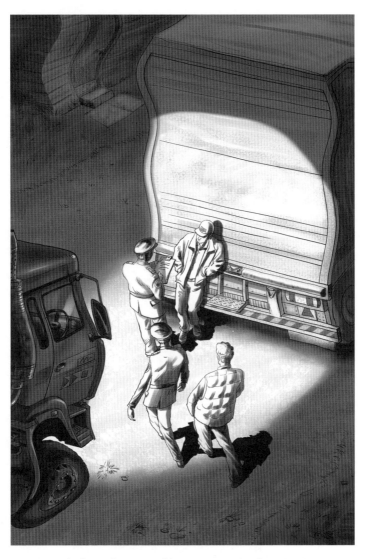

*The lorry driver would see a man in uniform (Ian)
interviewing a truck driver (Malc).*

Vehicle Check Area. When he got there, the driver would see a man in uniform (Ian) interviewing a truck driver (Malc). That way the real driver wouldn't think anything strange was going on; it was just normal Department of Transport interviews.

'It worked,' Ian says. 'That's what's so amazing. The driver brought his lorry up to the roundabout, stopped it, and got out. Tony comes driving up, gets out of his car, says he wants to check the cargo.'

The detective has a question. 'Suppose the cargo had been bananas or fish or something?'

'We send that lorry on, and stop another one, until we get something we can sell. But we were lucky first time. Washing machines, twenty-four of them, three hundred pounds each. We just got them into our own truck, and away we went.' Ian stops. 'You're wondering about the driver, aren't you? There were three of us, remember. We just tied him up, left him in his lorry. We knew he'd get free in the end.

'Tony had two lock-up garages, and we took the washing machines there. We were already thinking about who we could sell them to. There's a man we knew, name of Andy Horrigan, who does bits of business, doesn't ask questions, you know. I thought maybe he'd be interested. We wanted to be careful who we sold to, see. When the news got out about the robbery on the A90 . . .' Ian stops again for a minute. 'Of course, we'd already made our big mistake . . .'

One mistake. Ian asks for another cigarette. His hand is shaking as he lights it. He can't get it out of his head, the huge bad luck of it.

Before he's said a word to Andy Horrigan, Horrigan has a question for him.

'Here, Ian, heard anything about a robbery on the A90? Washing machines. Off the back of a lorry.'

'I didn't see anything in the newspapers,' Ian had said, which was true. All three of them had been surprised by that. Why hadn't the robbery been in the news? Ian could see that Horrigan knew the reason why, and Ian could also see in Horrigan's face that it wasn't good news.

'It wasn't in the newspapers, and it never will be,' says Horrigan. He goes on to explain why, and Ian feels his life coming to an end. He runs to the lock-up garage, finding Tony there. Tony already knows; it's written on his face. They have to move the washing machines, throw them away, somehow, somewhere, fast. But they don't have the truck any more. Where can they get a truck?

'Wait a bit,' Tony had said, starting to think again. 'Eddie Hart doesn't want the washing machines, does he? He only wants what he put in them.'

Eddie Hart. The name made Ian's legs go weak. 'Steady Eddie' was Mr Big in Dundee, a man who controlled most of the criminal business in the town. The stories about him would make your hair stand on end. If you made Steady Eddie angry, you didn't wake up again the next day. And now, Horrigan had said, Eddie was looking for blood.

He was in the drugs business, and needed to move drugs around a lot. What he did was this. He hid the drugs in fridges, washing machines, dryers, freezers, and his lorries went up and down the country. All they needed was a few false papers. It just so happened that Tony had stopped one of Eddie's drivers. And now Eddie wanted blood.

But Tony was right. Find the drugs, get them back to Eddie, and maybe Eddie wouldn't kill them. So they started pulling the packing out of the washing machines, taking the backs off, searching for hidden packets. They went through every machine, in both garages, checked them once, twice, three times. And found nothing.

'Wait a bit,' said Tony. He started counting the machines. There was one missing. The brothers looked at each other, then ran to Tony's car.

At Malc's mother's house, Malc had just fitted her new washing machine. Malc's mother was as pleased as anything. She had a crowd of neighbours in her kitchen. 'My boy's so good to me,' she was telling them. 'He saved his money and bought me this as a surprise.'

Even Ian knew they were in real trouble now. Everyone in town would get to hear about the new washing machines . . . and everyone meant Eddie Hart.

Tony and Ian took Malc outside and explained. Malc went back inside, pulled the machine out again, and started taking the back off. His hands were shaking so much, it took him a long time. But at last he had the back off, and began to pass brown- paper packets to Tony and Ian. Tony explained to the neighbours that these were just heavy things used in packing, to stop the machines shaking in the lorry.

'Like bricks?' one neighbour asked, and when Tony agreed with her, sweat running down his face, she added another question. 'Why cover bricks in brown paper?'

Malc began to pass brown-paper packets to Tony and Ian, and Tony explained that these were just heavy things used in packing.

Tony, beyond explanations, put his head in his hands and wept.

The detective brings back two cups of coffee, one for himself, one for Ian. He's been checking things, using the computer, making some phone calls. Ian sits ready to tell him the end of the story.

'We had to think of a way to get the drugs back to Eddie. He has a nightclub in Dundee. We drove up there, night before last, and put the drugs in one of the rubbish skips at the back of the club. Then we phoned the club and told them where to find the packets. The problem was that their rubbish skips are emptied at night. So sometime that night, the skip got emptied. And . . . and it was me who made the phone call . . . and there were two numbers in the phone-book. I meant to phone the office number, but I got it wrong and phoned the other number, which is a phone by the bar. Anyway, someone answered, I said my piece, and put the phone down. Maybe it was a customer, maybe they went outside and got the drugs for themselves before the skip was emptied . . . maybe they thought I was crazy or something . . .' Ian's voice is shaking, he's almost crying.

'So Mr Hart didn't get his drugs back?' the detective guesses. Ian nods. 'And now your brother and Malc have gone missing?'

'Eddie's got them,' says Ian. 'He must have.'

'And so you want us to protect you?' the detective asks.

'I'm in terrible danger,' Ian says. 'I mean, there's a price on my head now. You've *got* to help me!'

'I'm in terrible danger,' Ian says. 'I mean, there's a price on my head now. You've got to help me!'

The detective shakes his head. 'If somebody needs protection, we can do it,' he says. 'But there's no report of a robbery of washing machines on the A90. Yes, we would love to catch Mr Hart and put him in prison. But there's nothing to *prove* that Mr Hart is doing anything criminal.' The detective moves his chair closer to Ian. 'You see, I know that you lost your job after arguing with your boss, and you told your boss that your brother would come and break his bones. I found that out from the computer. What I didn't find in the computer was anything about washing machines, drugs in brown-paper packets, or missing persons.'

Ian jumps up from his seat, begins walking around the room. 'You could go to the place where they empty the rubbish skips. If the drugs are there, you'll find them. Or . . . or go to the garages, the washing machines will still be there . . . unless Steady Eddie's taken them. Don't you see? I'm the only one left who can speak against him!'

The detective is on his feet now, too. 'I think it's time for you to go home, son. I'll take you to the door.'

'I need protection!'

The detective comes up to him again, his face very close to Ian's.

'Get your brother to protect you. His name's . . . Billy, isn't it? The one who breaks bones. Only you can't do that, can you? Because you haven't got a brother called Billy. Or a brother called Tony.' The detective stops, begins again. 'You haven't got *anybody*, Ian. You're a nobody. These stories of yours – that's all they are, stories. Come on now, it's time you were home. Your mum will be worried about you.'

'She got a new washing machine last week,' Ian says softly. 'The man who brought it to the house, he said he was late because he'd had to stop at a checkpoint . . .'

It is quiet in the interview room. Quiet for a long time, until Ian begins weeping, weeping for the brother that he's just lost again.

The Day I met Sean Connery

SUSIE MAGUIRE

A story from Scotland, retold by Jennifer Bassett

Everybody has a dream person in their life, someone you think is wonderful, amazing, fantastic. Maybe it's a famous footballer, or an artist, a rock star, a scientist, an actor . . . You dream about meeting them, saving them from danger, even falling in love with them.

Marina has a dream person in her life, a perfect man. She never expects to meet him, or to talk to him . . .

Nobody believes me. Nobody. They just give me these funny looks, and say, 'oh yeah, right, Marina', like I'm a wee child telling lies to make herself important.

But maybe they don't *want* to believe me. Maybe they just wish they were brave enough to do something like that. Like my friend Agnes, she goes crazy if you talk about Tom Cruise. Veronica's just the same. She says her heart starts beating faster if she just *thinks* about Kevin Costner. She used to be crazy about some other Hollywood actor, but now she prefers older men, she says.

I agree with her. Young men are useless. There was this boy at Veronica's party, he just stood in the hall smoking with all his stupid friends, and never danced once – not once! Older men aren't stupid like that. OK, sometimes they're going a bit bald, or getting a bit fat, but if you don't mind that, they're actually a lot more interesting.

And that's how I feel about Sean Connery. I've always thought he was fantastic. My mum used to go crazy over him in all those old James Bond films, but I don't have a problem with that. I think Sean is . . . well, special. I mean, he's so much more interesting than a lot of actors. He's got a wife who's a famous artist, he speaks foreign languages, and . . . I don't know. He's got this deep, deep voice, and he's *funny* – not in a stupid way like the boys down the road, but funny in this really quiet, clever way. Everything about him is just right – a perfect man.

So, this is what happened. I was at the BBC television building in Glasgow. They've got a BBC bookshop in there and I went in to buy a book for my mum's birthday. In the hall as you go through to the bookshop there's a big television, and I stopped to watch it because the Glasgow news was on – and I heard his name! On the news it said that Sean Connery was coming to Scotland to do something, open a new children's hospital, something like that. And the BBC was going to film it – *today*!

I looked around at all the people in the hall, and they're just standing there, looking bored – *bored*, and Sean Connery is going to be *here in this building* at two o'clock! I couldn't believe it.

Just suppose, I thought, just suppose I'm standing here when he walks in. I decided I had to go and look at myself in a mirror, to see if my hair was standing on end, or my eyes had turned purple or something.

So I went through these doors and along a corridor, looking for the ladies' toilet. People went past, hurrying here and there, but nobody looked at me. I found the toilet, went in, and put on some more eye-shadow. Veronica says eye-shadow makes me look like a film star, so I put on lots.

I came out and went down another corridor, saw a lift, went up to the next floor, got out, turned left, and found the BBC restaurant. It was just for the people who worked there, of course, but I went in, got a tray, and bought this really nice meal for about 5p. Fantastic food. But the coffee was awful, truly awful. I sat there for an hour, but nobody asked me who I was, or what I was doing there. People came and went with their trays – you should see what unhealthy things some of them eat! It's not surprising that television people are all dead by the time they're forty-three.

Anyway, I was still sitting there when four men came with their trays and sat down at the table next to me. They all had big beards and long grey hair, and they started talking about making some film or other. One of them wanted this actor, another wanted a different actor. They didn't agree about anything, except that the coffee was awful, and that Scotland wouldn't win the big football match on Saturday. Then one of them said something about Sean.

'Yeah, they've sent a car to fetch him from his hotel, and he'll be here in about five minutes.'

They all got up to go, and so did I. I followed the man who had talked about Sean. He went along corridors, down

*I went in, got a tray, and bought
this really nice meal for about 5p.*

stairs, through doors, saying Hi to everybody he met. At last he went through these doors that said STUDIO TWO. There was a red light, and notices saying IF LIGHT IS RED, DO NOT ENTER. But he'd gone in, so I did too.

The studio was huge, with hundreds of people moving lights around, and a big blonde woman wearing headphones. I took a notebook out of my bag, and stood in a dark corner, and tried to look like an unimportant BBC person. The lights came on, went off, came on. They were showing bits of different Sean Connery films, but I couldn't hear the words.

Anyway, I was looking at my watch, when in he came. Sean. Mr Connery. He looked great. Just everyday clothes, but they were the best. There was a little crowd of people round him, and I had this wonderful idea. Suppose I just went along at the back of the crowd . . .

So that's what I did. We all went along this corridor, with Sean and a grey-haired man in front, talking about the filming. Sean was just giving one-word answers, and didn't sound very happy. Then we came to the lift. Sean and the grey-haired man got in, but it was only a small lift and the others turned away to find the stairs. But not me. I put my foot in the lift door, smiled, and said, 'Going up?'

Honestly, I don't know *how* I did it. But there I was, standing right next to Sean Connery. He was very, *very,* VERY tall. I just had a few minutes to stare at the middle bits of him out of the corner of my eye, and smell his aftershave. Then the lift stopped. I stood back, meaning 'you go first', but he did that thing with his eyebrows that makes you go funny inside, and said, 'Ladies first'.

How I got out of that lift, I do not know. My legs didn't seem to belong to me, and they wouldn't walk properly. Sean and the man went past me down the corridor, and I heard the man say something about tea and make-up. They went through a door at the end of the corridor.

I started to think, what am I doing here? What do I want? If I get to talk to him, what am I going to say? Then I had my great idea. Shortbread . . .

He lives in Spain now so he must really miss shortbread. I ran like crazy down the stairs to the restaurant on the first floor. I got a tray full of tea, real milk, sugar, and a plate of good Scottish-made pieces of shortbread. I carried it very slowly to the lift, went up to the fourth floor, and down the corridor. I took a deep breath, and knocked on the door.

He said, 'Come in.'

So in I went, and he was sitting at a kind of Hollywood-type table, with millions of lights round the mirror, in some very nice trousers and a white shirt, combing his moustache. Our eyes met in the mirror, and I nearly died.

He said, 'Ah, tea.'

'Or coffee, if you prefer,' I said.

'BBC coffee is always terrible,' he said, with this wee smile, and I nodded, to show I agreed, which I did.

I poured him the tea, moved the milk and sugar closer, and pushed the plate of shortbread right under his nose.

'Expect you've not had this for a wee while,' I said. 'Go on, put some in your pocket for later, I always get hungry when I'm trying to go to sleep and have to get a biscuit.'

I wasn't brave enough to look at him – suppose he just

disappeared, right in front of my eyes! But he laughed a bit, and I did look, and he has these amazing eyes, deep, deep eyes, and suddenly it's like flying off the top of a mountain. I just felt a big whoosh – like: I Have Met Sean Connery and I Can Do Anything. Amazing. Unbelievable.

Anyway, that was very nearly the last word that I had with him, because right then the door opened and another tea tray appeared. No shortbread. There was this big silence when the woman carrying it saw me, and then she just smiled and opened her mouth and shut it a few times. In the end she just shook her head, like she was saying, 'OK, you win,' and went out of the door. I think my face showed the true story because Sean gave me a funny look. Then *he* poured *me* a cup of tea.

Anyway, I had to tell him, in the end. I just couldn't pretend any longer, you know. But he was very nice. He didn't shout at me, or phone for help, or lock me in a cupboard. He just looked at me, just – looked.

And then he said, 'Why?'

And I went, 'Why? Why, Sean? Don't you realize by now that there are millions of women who will never meet anyone as good-looking as you, or as funny? Millions of women who have to live with boring ordinary men. *You* are different, special, one of a kind.'

I probably went on a bit. I told him about myself, and my last boyfriend, and how that had finished, and how I didn't know what to do. Should I go to college, not go to college?

He raised the eyebrows like he was trying not to laugh. I didn't mind. It was great just talking to him like a normal

He raised the eyebrows like he was trying not to laugh.
I didn't mind. It was great just talking to him.

person. And he gave me lots of good advice, which I'm not going to tell anyone. He talked to me about sport, and what he thought about Kevin Costner. I can't tell Veronica!

Finally, there was another knock on the door, and the grey-haired man came in, looked at me, and went 'Aah Aah'. And that's when I knew my time was over, so I put my hand out, and Sean stood up and shook it, and said, 'It was nice talking to you . . .' and I said 'Marina, Marina McLoughlin, very pleasant talking to you also, Sean.' Then he turned to the man, and said, 'Kenneth?', and I waved goodbye, and backed out of the door. And then I ran like crazy.

Anyway, that's the story about how I met Sean Connery. Veronica and Agnes just say, 'Rubbish'. I nearly phoned Michael, my ex-boyfriend, but you know, something stopped me, and I think it was that big whoosh I'd got off Sean. I thought no, I don't have to accept less than the best. Who cares about Michael and his boring bike and his boring beer? I can do better than that.

GLOSSARY

aftershave a liquid with a nice smell that men put on their faces
amazing very surprising
aspirin a medicine that stops pain
blouse a shirt for a woman
brick a small block of baked clay; bricks are used for building
bucket a round metal container with a handle, for carrying water
camp (prison) a place where prisoners of war are kept
cardigan a soft jacket, usually made of wool
cargo things carried by lorries, ships, planes, etc.
cattle cows that are kept for their milk or meat; **Highland cattle** are a kind of cattle found in the Scottish highlands
cave a large hole in the side of a hill or cliff
cheek the soft part of the face below the eye
cheer *(v & n)* to make someone feel happy; happiness
confession when someone says that they have done something bad or wrong
corridor a long narrow walkway inside a building
croft a small, simple house or farm, especially in Scotland
drug an illegal substance that people take because it makes them feel happy or excited
dust dry dirt, like powder
ferry a boat that takes people on short journeys across a river or the sea
fever when your body is very hot and painful because you are ill
Fionn & Ossian heroes of ancient Scottish and Irish stories
First Aid medical help for someone who is hurt
first-footing being the first person to enter somebody's house in the new year (a Scottish custom)

fool a person who does something silly, not sensible; *(adj)* **foolish**
Gaelic the Celtic language of Scotland
Hogmanay in Scotland, New Year's Eve (31 December)
huge very, very big
hut a small simple building with one room
lamb a young sheep
lamp a thing that gives light
ledge a long narrow flat place, for example, under a window
loch in Scotland, a lake, or a small bit of sea almost surrounded
   by land
lorry a large vehicle for carrying cargo on the roads
magic when strange or impossible things seem to happen
mainland the main area of land of a country, not its islands
make up (in this story) special creams for actors to put on the
   face
nightclub a place for drinking and dancing at night
oar a long stick with a flat end used for moving a boat through
   water
och *(Scottish English)* an expression of surprise
ordinary not special or unusual
peat a substance from the earth, used for burning on fires
pension money from the government when you are old and do
   not work any more
pit a mine; a deep hole in the ground where coal is taken out
protect *(v)* to keep somebody or something safe; *(n)* **protection**
roundabout a place where roads meet and cars must drive round
   a circle
scullery a small room next to the kitchen in an old house
shameful making you feel ashamed
shilling 5 pence in old British money (before 1971)
shore the land along the edge of the sea

shortbread   a rich biscuit (cookie) made with a lot of butter

signpost   a sign beside a road, that shows the way to a place

skip *(n)*   a very large container for rubbish

slip-road   a road used for driving on or off a major road

spirit   the part of a person that is not the body, and that perhaps lives after death

sweat *(n)*   liquid that comes through your skin when you are hot

tease   to laugh at someone in a friendly way

tide   the movement of the sea towards the land, and away from it

torch   a small electric light you can carry in the hand

tray   a flat object you can use for carrying food or drinks

truck   a vehicle used for carrying cargo

wardrobe   a tall cupboard for clothes

wee *(Scottish English)*   very small

weep   to cry, because you are sad

ye *(Scottish English)*   you

ACTIVITIES

Before Reading

Before you read the stories, read the introductions at the beginning, then use these activities to help you think about the stories. How much can you guess or predict?

1 *The Pigeon* (story introduction page 1). Can you guess why Jan feels this way about a sick pigeon? Choose the answer you like best.

   1 It's because nobody took care of Jan when he was a child.
   2 It's because he lost someone very dear to him.
   3 It's because he loves all animals and birds.
   4 It's because he is lonely and has no one else to love.

2 *Donald and the Drovers* (story introduction page 13). What do you know about fords? Use the words below to complete the passage (one word for each gap).

boat, dangerous, drowned, faster, high, island, low, quickly, tide, walk

At _____ tide on these Scottish fords, it is possible to _____ across from one _____ to the next. But it is _____ to be on the ford when the _____ is coming in because the sea moves very _____ across the sand. It moves much _____ than a man can run, and people have _____ on these fords. At _____ tide it is necessary to take a _____ across the ford.

3 *Andrina* (story introduction page 21). Why does Captain Torvald try to forget his past? Can you guess? Choose one or more of these ideas.

1 Captain Torvald was a bad seaman, and because of him a ship was lost and many people drowned.
2 He murdered someone.
3 He was once very cruel to a girl who loved him.
4 He left his wife and children and ran away with a younger woman.

4 *The Confession* (story introduction page 36). How do you think the interview will go? Choose one of these possibilities.

1 Ian tells the truth. The detective . . .
a) believes him.   b) doesn't believe him.
2 Ian doesn't tell the truth. The detective . . .
a) knows he is lying.   b) doesn't realize he is lying.

5 *The Day I Met Sean Connery* (story introduction page 48). How many of these things happen in Marina's story? Choose **Y** (yes) or **N** (no) for each idea.

Marina meets Sean Connery . . .
1 and they have a nice long talk.   Y / N
2 but he only says three words to her.   Y / N
3 and makes him laugh.   Y / N
4 and he falls in love with her.   Y / N
5 and knocks a cup of coffee over him.   Y / N
6 and cannot speak because she is so excited.   Y / N

62

After Reading

1 **Here are the thoughts of five characters (one from each story). Which characters are they, and from which story? Who or what are they thinking about?**

1 'We've missed the tide! But we need to get across tonight, so that means taking the boat. I wonder what the old boatman will ask for the fare? Well, he'll not get more than three pence from me!'

2 'Who was that, then? I looked really silly, coming in with a *second* tea tray. She doesn't work in the restaurant, that's for sure. I've never seen her before. And there she was, with her tea tray, talking away to him like an old friend!'

3 'I'm getting bored listening to all this rubbish. There's not a word of truth in it. I've got other work to do, reports to write. It's time to finish and send the boy home. I feel sorry for his mother . . .'

4 'Oh, the poor, dear man. He's having one of his bad times again. I always know. I can see it in his face, and his sad eyes. It's best to leave him alone for a while . . .'

5 'The old man didn't look too well tonight, not at all. Drinking a lot of whisky, and having these fever dreams about a girl! But I wish I hadn't laughed at him now. There was a confused look on his face I've never seen before . . .'

2 Here is Ella, telling her son about her Jan's past. Complete the sentences for her. Use as many words as you like.

'You see, Robert, terrible things have _____. He had a family before, a wife and a _____. In the war they were put into different prison camps, and when Jan came out, he _____. He learnt that his wife _____, and he looked for _____. At last he found a girl who told him _____. The poor, poor things. He still _____, you know.'

3 Captain Torvald talked to both Tina Stewart and Isaac Irving about Andrina. What did they think about it? Complete their opinions with these words (one word for each gap).

called / dreams / explain / family / fever / ghost / imagine / imagines / message / name / never / nurse / sensible / whisky

TINA STEWART: There is nobody _____ Andrina on this island, and _____ has been. I know the history of every _____ here. No, I think the Captain saw a _____. He's a _____ man and he doesn't _____ things. Somebody, or something, is trying to send him a _____ from the dead.'

ISAAC IRVING: It's very easy to _____ it. The Captain was ill, with a bad _____, and I expect he had a few glasses of _____ too. Everyone would like a kind _____ when they are ill. So in his _____ the Captain _____ a sweet young woman and gives her the _____ of Andrina.'

4 Do you think Captain Torvald replied to Sigrid's letter from Australia? Give your opinion, and explain your reasons for it.

5 Here are two conversations that happened after the ends of the
   stories, between Ian and his mother, and between Marina and
   her friend Veronica. Match each question with an answer, then
   put them into two separate conversations.

QUESTIONS

   1 'OK, you went up in the lift with him. And what did you
      do after that?'

   2 'You've been out a long time, Ian. Where have you been?'

   3 'Oh no, not again! Confession about what? You haven't
      done anything, you've got nothing to confess!'

   4 'You just walked into his room? Didn't he say "Who are
      you?" or "Go away"?'

   5 'And I suppose you told him you had a brother too. Did he
      believe you? Did he believe any of it?'

   6 'I don't believe you! What kind of advice? Tell me!'

ANSWERS

   7 'Yes, I have. I was confessing about the stolen washing
      machines. And the drugs. I told the detective everything.'

   8 'No, he didn't! We had tea, and talked. And he gave me lots
      of good advice, about life, and boyfriends.'

   9 'I've been at the police station, making my confession.'

  10 'No, if you don't believe me, I won't say another word! I
      certainly won't tell you what he said about Kevin Costner.'

  11 'No, he didn't. He told me to go home. He doesn't
      understand. *You* don't understand. *Nobody* understands . . .'

  12 'I had this great idea. I got a tray with tea and shortbread
      biscuits, took it to his room, and went in.'

6 Which famous person would you like to meet, and why? Imagine you are, like Marina, in a lift with this person. How will you begin a conversation? Think of the best two questions to ask.

Question 1: _____

Question 2: _____

7 Here is a short poem (a kind of poem called a haiku) about one of the stories. Which of the five stories is it about?

> *Old year, new year, still*
> *the pain of a distant death*
> *breaks his heart in two.*

Here is another haiku. Which story is this one about?

> *His eyebrows go up.*
> *He is trying not to laugh.*
> *Nice girl. Nice shortbread.*

A haiku is a Japanese poem, which is always in three lines, and the three lines always have 5, 7, and 5 syllables each, like this:

| Old | year | new | year | still | = 5 syllables
| the | pain | of | a | dis | tant | death | = 7 syllables
| breaks | his | heart | in | two | = 5 syllables

Now write your own haiku, one for each story. Think about what each story is really about. What are the important ideas for you? Remember to keep to three lines of 5, 7, 5 syllables each.

ABOUT THE AUTHORS

EONA MACNICOL

Eona Kathleen Macnicol (1910–2002) was born in Inverness, in Scotland. As a child, she often stayed in her parents' village of Abriachan, in the hills above Loch Ness, and many of her short stories draw on her Gaelic childhood. She studied English at Edinburgh University, and trained as a teacher in Cambridge. For a while she taught in Dublin, then in Kalimpong among the foothills of the Himalayas, and also in Madras.

She wrote two novels and many short stories. *The Hallowe'en Hero and Other Stories* (1969) described the old days in the Scottish Highlands. *The Jail Dancing and other stories of an old Scottish town* (1978) described life in Inverness. The story *The Pigeon* comes from *A Carver of Coal* (1979), stories set in a modern mining village in the south of Scotland.

MALCOLM LAING

Malcolm Laing (1888–1968) was born on the Isle of North Uist in the Outer Hebrides. He studied at Glasgow University, received an M.A. degree, and then qualified as a Church of Scotland minister. For the next fifty years he worked as a parish minister; twenty-one of these years were spent on South Uist.

In the 1930s and 40s he wrote poetry in both Gaelic and English, some of which was published, and in the 1950s he began to write short stories. *Donald and the Drovers* (1956) was published in *The Chambers's Journal*, and he read many of his Gaelic stories on BBC Radio Scotland.

He was a keen fly fisher on the lochs of South Uist, and made many crossings on the South Ford. He knew its dangers well, and more than once was caught by the incoming tide.

GEORGE MACKAY BROWN

George Mackay Brown (1921–1996) was born in Stromness in the Orkney Isles, in Scotland. Apart from a few years studying in Edinburgh, he spent his life in Stromness. He had very poor health, had little money, and lived a quiet, simple life. He never married, and after his parents died, he lived alone.

He was one of Scotland's greatest lyric poets, and his poems, stories, and novels brought him world-wide fame. Visitors from Europe, America, and Asia came to knock at his door every summer. But if they came too early, they would find a notice on the door saying 'Not at home'. He always was at home, of course, sitting in the kitchen for his daily three hours of writing.

His first book of poetry, *The Storm,* was published in 1954. Fifteen more poetry collections followed, and nine volumes of short stories, including *Andrina and Other Stories* (1983). He also wrote novels, plays, essays, and children's stories.

Mackay Brown disliked the modern world, and his works explore the long and ancient history of Orkney, its myths, and its culture, transforming the familiar world into something timeless and universal. The poet's 'true task', he wrote in one of his poems, is the 'interrogation of silence'.

IAN RANKIN

Ian Rankin (1960–) was born in Fife, in Scotland. He graduated from Edinburgh University in 1982, and then spent three years writing novels when he was supposed to be studying for a Ph.D. in Scottish Literature. His first novel was published in 1987, and since then he has become an international bestselling crime writer. He has won many awards and honorary degrees, and in 2002 was awarded the OBE for services to literature.

He is most famous for his seventeen *Inspector Rebus* novels, many of which have been filmed for television. The series began with *Knots and Crosses* in 1987 and ended with *Exit Music* in 2007, when Inspector Rebus retired from the Edinburgh police, to the great sadness of Ian Rankin's readers. The city of Edinburgh itself is as much of a character as John Rebus, and Ian Rankin has said, 'I owe a great debt to Robert Louis Stevenson and to the city of his birth. In a way they both changed my life . . . Without Dr Jekyll and Mr Hyde I might never have come up with Detective Inspector John Rebus.'

SUSIE MAGUIRE

Susie Maguire (1958–) was born in Edinburgh, Scotland. In her working life she has been many things – an actor, a comedy performer, singer, and TV presenter. While she was performing in comedy clubs in the 1980s, she created the character of Marina McLoughlin, a naive young woman from Glasgow with a taste for adventure. This is the same Marina as in *The Day I Met Sean Connery*. The story has been adapted both for radio and television, and Marina will soon appear again in a novel.

Susie Maguire is the author of two short-story collections, *The Short Hello* (2000) and *Furthermore* (2005), and a collection of poems, *How to Hug* (2009). She says she likes short stories 'because they're short; that is their beauty. Because they're intense, satisfying to write and to read. I like to see how much I can show in how few words . . .'

OXFORD BOOKWORMS LIBRARY

Classics • Crime & Mystery • Factfiles • Fantasy & Horror
Human Interest • Playscripts • Thriller & Adventure
True Stories • World Stories

The OXFORD BOOKWORMS LIBRARY provides enjoyable reading in English, with a wide range of classic and modern fiction, non-fiction, and plays. It includes original and adapted texts in seven carefully graded language stages, which take learners from beginner to advanced level. An overview is given on the next pages.

All Stage 1 titles are available as audio recordings, as well as over eighty other titles from Starter to Stage 6. All Starters and many titles at Stages 1 to 4 are specially recommended for younger learners. Every Bookworm is illustrated, and Starters and Factfiles have full-colour illustrations.

The OXFORD BOOKWORMS LIBRARY also offers extensive support. Each book contains an introduction to the story, notes about the author, a glossary, and activities. Additional resources include tests and worksheets, and answers for these and for the activities in the books. There is advice on running a class library, using audio recordings, and the many ways of using Oxford Bookworms in reading programmes. Resource materials are available on the website <www.oup.com/bookworms>.

The *Oxford Bookworms Collection* is a series for advanced learners. It consists of volumes of short stories by well-known authors, both classic and modern. Texts are not abridged or adapted in any way, but carefully selected to be accessible to the advanced student.

You can find details and a full list of titles in the *Oxford Bookworms Library Catalogue* and *Oxford English Language Teaching Catalogues*, and on the website <www.oup.com/bookworms>.

THE OXFORD BOOKWORMS LIBRARY
GRADING AND SAMPLE EXTRACTS

STARTER • 250 HEADWORDS

present simple – present continuous – imperative –
can/cannot, must – *going to* (future) – simple gerunds ...

Her phone is ringing – but where is it?

Sally gets out of bed and looks in her bag. No phone.
She looks under the bed. No phone. Then she looks behind
the door. There is her phone. Sally picks up her phone and
answers it. *Sally's Phone*

STAGE 1 • 400 HEADWORDS

... past simple – coordination with *and, but, or* –
subordination with *before, after, when, because, so* ...

I knew him in Persia. He was a famous builder and I
worked with him there. For a time I was his friend, but
not for long. When he came to Paris, I came after him –
I wanted to watch him. He was a very clever, very dangerous
man. *The Phantom of the Opera*

STAGE 2 • 700 HEADWORDS

... present perfect – *will* (future) – *(don't) have to, must not, could* –
comparison of adjectives – simple *if* clauses – past continuous –
tag questions – *ask/tell* + infinitive ...

While I was writing these words in my diary, I decided
what to do. I must try to escape. I shall try to get down the
wall outside. The window is high above the ground, but
I have to try. I shall take some of the gold with me – if I
escape, perhaps it will be helpful later. *Dracula*

STAGE 3 • 1000 HEADWORDS

... should, may – present perfect continuous – *used to* – past perfect – causative – relative clauses – indirect statements ...

Of course, it was most important that no one should see Colin, Mary, or Dickon entering the secret garden. So Colin gave orders to the gardeners that they must all keep away from that part of the garden in future. *The Secret Garden*

STAGE 4 • 1400 HEADWORDS

... past perfect continuous – passive (simple forms) – *would* conditional clauses – indirect questions – relatives with *where/when* – gerunds after prepositions/phrases ...

I was glad. Now Hyde could not show his face to the world again. If he did, every honest man in London would be proud to report him to the police. *Dr Jekyll and Mr Hyde*

STAGE 5 • 1800 HEADWORDS

... future continuous – future perfect – passive (modals, continuous forms) – *would have* conditional clauses – modals + perfect infinitive ...

If he had spoken Estella's name, I would have hit him. I was so angry with him, and so depressed about my future, that I could not eat the breakfast. Instead I went straight to the old house. *Great Expectations*

STAGE 6 • 2500 HEADWORDS

... passive (infinitives, gerunds) – advanced modal meanings – clauses of concession, condition

When I stepped up to the piano, I was confident. It was as if I knew that the prodigy side of me really did exist. And when I started to play, I was so caught up in how lovely I looked that I didn't worry how I would sound. *The Joy Luck Club*

MORE WORLD STORIES FROM BOOKWORMS

The Meaning of Gifts: Stories from Turkey
STAGE 1   RETOLD BY JENNIFER BASSETT

—

Cries from the Heart: Stories from Around the World*
STAGE 2   RETOLD BY JENNIFER BASSETT

Changing their Skies: Stories from Africa
STAGE 2   RETOLD BY JENNIFER BASSETT

—

The Long White Cloud: Stories from New Zealand
STAGE 3   RETOLD BY CHRISTINE LINDOP

Dancing with Strangers: Stories from Africa*
STAGE 3   RETOLD BY CLARE WEST

Playing with Fire: Stories from the Pacific Rim*
STAGE 3   RETOLD BY JENNIFER BASSETT

Leaving No Footprint: Stories from Asia
STAGE 3   RETOLD BY CLARE WEST

—

Doors to a Wider Place: Stories from Australia
STAGE 4   RETOLD BY CHRISTINE LINDOP

Land of my Childhood: Stories from South Asia**
STAGE 4   RETOLD BY CLARE WEST

The Price of Peace: Stories from Africa
STAGE 4   RETOLD BY CHRISTINE LINDOP

—

Treading on Dreams: Stories from Ireland
STAGE 5   RETOLD BY CLARE WEST

** Winner: Language Learner Literature Awards

* Finalist: Language Learner Literature Awards